Jobless Cash

How to Make Money if You're Unemployed or Just Plain Tired of Working for Someone Else

By Omar Johnson

I0462552

Table of Contents

Introduction

How important is money in your life? For most
of us, money is one of the most important
aspects in life. Money allows us to live the kind
of life we want, to be able to eat, afford shelter
over our heads, go on vacations, have some of
the luxuries that we want in life, and much
more. If you don't have money, life can become
very difficult and it can lead to excessive stress,
physical health problems, broken relationships,
and much more.

Even though you know and understand the
value of money, what happens when you're

unable to earn it? What happens when you lose your job or a career you've chosen isn't providing you with enough money to live the kind of life that you want? You may have enough money to buy food and pay the rent, but is that enough?

Everywhere you turn today, you can see the signs of frustration that people have because they are either without a job or working for a company or in a career that does not fulfill them. The economy has not shown the kind of signs of improvement that the government would like us to believe is occurring. So while you are waiting for more opportunities to arise, the hours and days of your life are passing you by.

Some people will say that money is the root of all evil. However, money doesn't actually have any power. It is only a representation of the value that we place on merchandise or ourselves. So how much are you worth? Do you value yourself, your time, and your effort far more than what you are getting back from your job? Do you value yourself more than someone who is sitting around applying for jobs and being unable to get a quality job offer?

If so, you are not alone. There are millions of people in the United States alone right now, at this moment, feeling the same frustration and pain that you are. These are people who at some point in their lives wanted more than what they have at this moment. But how do you get more if you don't have work or you are working for an employer with limited opportunities?

The answer is to take charge of your life and your income. I know that some of you will say that's easier to say than to do, and in some cases you are right. However, there are a number of opportunities that exist that can help you change your life and take charge of your income.

Imagine the Possibilities

I want you to take a moment and imagine the possibilities. Imagine that you woke up one morning knowing what you are going to be doing for the day. Imagine that you woke up and knew that you had the opportunity to make two, three, or even 10 times the amount of money you were making at your last job.

How does that feel? How does that concept strike you? I would expect that you would be thrilled at the prospect of being able to achieve that kind of money.

You're like most people, aren't you? You are saying, "How can I possibly make that kind of money if I don't even have a job right now?" Or you are saying, "Why would I expect to be able to make more money by myself than working for a major Fortune 2000 company?"

The only answer I can provide to those questions is another question: Why not?

If you open your eyes and look around, you will see tens of thousands of people working for themselves, doing jobs and taking advantage of the opportunities that exist all around them. These people, at one point, were just like you. They were either unemployed, disenfranchised, or simply frustrated that they could not make more money than they were earning and valued their time far more than their former employers did.

How do these people do it? They are not inventors, they are not snake oil salesman, and they are not superstar sports athletes that happen to have a talent beyond measure. These are people who were willing to do whatever it takes within the law and within their moral scope to improve their lot in life.

They were willing to do jobs that some other people may have scoffed at. Some of them may have been willing to wash windows for living. Some of them may have decided to set up websites and sell affiliate products through them. Some of them may have decided to become call-center assistants, you know the ones I'm talking about, the ones who answer the phone for companies when customers call with questions, comments, or complaints.

They are not the most glamorous opportunities in the world, but when you control your hours and your pay rate, the possibilities are almost endless.

So before we get into how to make money if you're unemployed or just plain tired of working for someone else, let me ask you one more question. Knowing what you know now, already, are there any limits that you would place on yourself for jobs that you would never even consider taking?

If so, that's fine. This book will highlight dozens of potential opportunities that exist everywhere around you. These are opportunities and assignments that companies and other individuals are willing to pay good money to be completed. If you want the most out of your life, and want the best chance to be compensated for the value that you offer, then keep reading this book.

If you'd prefer to simply complain that you don't have any money because you don't have a job, or that you don't have enough money because your job doesn't pay what you feel

you're worth, then all I can say to you is good

luck.

For the rest of us, let's get started.

1 – The Essence of Money

Money makes the world go round. This is a saying that has been in existence for a long, long time. But what does it mean?

What is money? And more importantly, how does it make the world go round? Before you can value money, you need to understand what it is at its root core. This is what is known as the essence of money.

Money is not actually a material object. The dollar bills in your wallet or the coins that are lost in the cushions of your couch don't actually have any inherent value. That kind of money is nothing more than a representation of value. Let me step back for a moment in time.

In the beginning of civilization, men traded for goods and services with what they had. If you needed shoes, you may have to trade a pig to the shoemaker for them. The shoemaker would need leather and other items to make more shoes, so he may end up trading that pig for the hide of cattle. That was the original essence of commerce in the world.

Then, during Roman times, the concept of money began to flourish. It was during this age when gold coins were forged and the same objects that had been traded for years for other objects were then assigned specific values based on supply, demand, and quality. Though shoes would no longer cost the price of a pig, they may cost one gold coin. The shoemaker may then have to pay two gold coins for the hide of a cattle.

Today, the concept of money is essentially the same. Take out any bill from your wallet, whether it is a $1 or $20 bill, and you will see a very specific statement on that bill. It reads: this note is legal tender for all debts, public and private. Now, legal tender is defined as, "Coins or bank notes that must be accepted if offered in payment of a debt."

So what does this mean? It means that the

dollars that you have represent a specific

amount of buying power. It represents value

that is determined by global and domestic

economic conditions. The more 'money' you

earn, the more valued your services are deemed.

However, the value of money rises and falls,

increasing or decreasing your purchasing power;

it is these factors that are beyond your control.

"But I don't have any debt," you may be saying.

If that is true then you are one of the lucky few

and I congratulate you for that. However, a debt

is not necessarily what we consider to be a debt.

If you go to a store and place a number of items

in your cart, you are essentially taking possession of those items. Now, when you get to the cash register, you have what is known as a debt for each of those items. You call it purchasing, but the federal treasury calls it settling a debt.

Now, let's talk about appreciating the value of money.

How to Appreciate Money

So how do you go about beginning to appreciate money? The first thing is to understand what money represents. Money represents a person's ability to acquire goods or services. But it also represents a person's value. We'll get more into your inherent value in a little while.

Our society no longer appreciates money. Even though millions of people are classified as either lower middle class or poor, they have more and have access to more than our grandparents or great-grandparents did that were classified as middle or upper middle class.

A lot of this is based on debt and the ability to acquire merchandise now while trying to pay for it later, with millions of people defaulting on their debts as well. But it is also the result of the increased demand of consumers for products that are cheaper. Cheaper made products are disposable and we live in a disposable society.

A disposable society simply cannot appreciate the value of money. When you cannot appreciate the value of money, you end up under appreciating the value of yourself. Money is not the root of all evil. Money does not make the world go round either. However, if you do not value money for what it is (the representation of value that allows you to purchase goods and services), then how can you expect to earn more than your making now, whether you are unemployed or working a full-time job?

The answer is simple: you cannot.

What I mean by that is: if you don't appreciate money, then no amount of money is going to make you feel full-filled. No job is going to bring you the satisfaction that you are doing enough and you are being compensated enough in terms of money. Learn to place true value on money and also keep it in its place.

Money will not bring you happiness. It will not bring you joy. It is harmful to undervalue money but it is equally harmful to overstate its power. Keep money in perspective.

How do we Value Money?

So how do we properly value money? The first step is to view it through the lens of history.

Money has been used to buy influence, acquire power, and simply to survive.

Your grandparents used it to build a better life for themselves and ultimately you. Your employer uses money to help grow his or her business as well as to signify which employees are more "valuable" to him or her.

The average person simply does not value money anymore. They know when they don't have it, but when they do, they don't know how to save or invest and begin to place a greater value on money than it deserves. For example, have you ever gone to the store without money and saw something that you wanted? Almost everyone has at least once in the past couple of weeks. Most of us have had the experience almost daily.

That is because we are surrounded by an endless stream of advertising and marketing by companies that spend millions of dollars every year to try to make us feel less worthy unless we purchase their products. We have become a materialistic society.

The only way to get out of that rut is to find peace within yourself to appreciate what you do have and not feel the need to have more in order to become happy. That is a long road to achieve, but is well worth the trip. It also leads to the more important facet which is learning to value yourself.

Value Yourself

How much do you value yourself? If you say that you value yourself a lot, do your actions support that claim? More likely than not your actions do not speak to yourself worth or value.

Every person has inherent value for themselves, their lives, and the people that they surround themselves with. Take a good look around you right now. Are the friends that you have worthy of you? Do they hold you back? Or do they propel you in a positive direction, do they encourage you to pursue your dreams or do they tell you, "You can't do that"?

If you surround yourself with people who say you can't do something, then you are not valuing yourself. If you do not value yourself properly, then why would you deserve more money? Whether you have a job or not, are not happy with the current pay rate or simply want more, how can you justify that if you do not value yourself enough to surround yourself with people who hold you in that same value?

Now, look around your personal space right at this moment. Is it neat and organized or are there dirty dishes, dirty sheets, papers everywhere, and just plain disorganization all around you? If you have a clean, neat, and organized space around you, then you value yourself enough to be worthy of earning more. If you fall into the latter category, however, then you don't value yourself enough.

What about the jobs that you have taken and held over the years? It doesn't matter if you are currently working or unemployed, if you have had jobs in the past, have they paid you what you felt that you are worth? If not, what did you do? Did you work harder in the hopes of getting a promotion or a raise? Or did you simply proceed to do just enough to get your paycheck and then go home and grumble about it to your friends?

The latter is the actions of a person who does not value himself. A person who values himself will constantly seek improvement in his or her life. When you value yourself, you will tend to demand more money for tasks that you perform, whether you offer services or generate products to sell. Money becomes the reward for your true value to a customer or company.

In order to truly understand how to make money when you are unemployed or just tired of working for someone else, you need to make sure that you understand your value and that you value money appropriately. When you do

that, the opportunities will begin to surround

you.

2 – Opportunities Surround You

Everywhere you look there are opportunities to make money. Most of the time however, we aren't paying attention to these types of opportunities. You may have thought that they were "beneath" you or your educational level. You may have thought that these types of opportunities were for more "desperate" people.

The reality is that anywhere that people are willing to spend money to have something done is an opportunity for you to make money. Even when you don't think people are willing to spend money on it, there is always the opportunity to make money doing it. The reason? It's because when you find someone who needs a service that you can provide but who isn't willing or able to pay you for your service, there are likely dozens who have money and would be willing to pay you for that service.

Dog walking. You might not think it, but dog walkers can make a very good living. These are individuals who tend to live in big cities where professional individuals live and have pets that require care while they are at work. You need to be trustworthy and honest and have a solid background, but for a few hours a day of going out and walking dogs, making sure that you clean up after them, you can make several hundred dollars.

Recycling. We often see people rummaging through garbage, pulling out cans and bottles, placing their filled bags in carts and pushing them to the store. Depending on where you live, that could be good money. It has helped more than a few people climb their way out of poverty and even homelessness. Some states make it much more profitable than others.

Coffee. There have been several cases of people beginning small businesses by selling coffee at high traffic congestion areas. Some of these activities are illegal and require permits from local jurisdictions, but if you are savvy enough, and know where traffic tends to come to a stop for a significant period of time, you too can join the fray of people who have made a lot of money this way. One man turned his idea and effort into a successful chain of cafes throughout New York City, all catering to the time-strapped consumer.

The point here is to make you start thinking about all of the different opportunities that exist around you at this moment. Perhaps you were raised to believe that getting a college degree and then working for a major corporation was the only legitimate way to make a living.

Perhaps your family won't see that a job that doesn't require any college to be worthwhile. The question you have to ask yourself in this instance is whether you want to be accepted by people who should accept you for whatever you do or whether you want to make money and have control over how much you make.

30 years ago, working for a major corporation was a viable concept. You'd work for them for 30 or 40 years and then retire with a pension. Today, that level of loyalty rarely exists anymore. Now companies are cutting back salaries and even cutting hours to help save money. You may become frustrated and angry

about this, but it has nothing to do with corporate greed, CEO pay, or even the benefits that employees receive. This has to do with you and your desire to take charge of your financial life.

Requires Effort

These opportunities that I have mentioned in brief and will mention in more detail later have one thing in common, no matter what they are. That is they require a significant level of effort on your part to make them succeed.

You cannot expect to go out, find a few opportunities, do a little bit of work for them, and make a ton of money. Very few people in this world have made a lot of money with very little effort. Those people might be considered lucky, but when you don't put in the effort, how can you truly value the work that you do or yourself in the end? Those kinds of people will always have questions about themselves and an emptiness that they cannot fill.

You absolutely must be willing to make a serious effort in your endeavors to make money.

"But I have been working hard my whole life and have nothing to show for it. Why are you talking to me about effort?"

I am only talking about the effort required because some people, when they are unemployed for a significant amount of time or have grown tired of putting in a tremendous amount of effort for somebody else, may be looking for the "easy" way out.

I am just making a point that there is no easy way out when it comes to making money. No matter what you do, where you live, what you want in life, you will need to make a serious effort to get the amount of money that you want.

As long as you are willing to make that kind of effort, there is nothing that will be able to keep you down unless YOU let it.

Limitless

The opportunities are limitless. The abundance that exists in our world extends far beyond our comprehension. No matter who you are, where you live, where you come from, what your ambitions or dreams are in life, you are bound by only one thing and that is you.

What are you willing to do to make money right now, to control the amount of money you make, and to become your own boss?

Never compromise your moral integrity or break the law, but beyond that, whatever you are willing to do, the steps you are willing to take, will determine how much opportunity truly exists for you and how much you will make.

So let's get into the meat and potatoes of this book and find some amazing ideas that you can start using right now to make cash and become the creator of your own destiny.

3 – Ideas for Making Quick Cash

We have now reached the heart of this book. I am going to show you a list of possible opportunities that you can do right now to make money. None of these opportunities require you to have a formal education or to be working at this moment. However, some of them may require some startup capital. There are ways to get around these prerequisites, but I will address them when they arise.

As I mentioned in the previous chapter, you will need to be determined to succeed and be willing to put in the effort from the beginning. Some of these ideas will require more physical exertion than mental exertion. Some of them will require more understanding of computer technology or design or some other facet. No matter what it is, you can advance yourself and increase your educational level on these topics by simply going online, doing a little homework, or even heading to the bookstore and reading a few books while you are there.

If you find any of these ideas "beneath" you, that is fine. However, I'm sure you will find at least a few ideas here that will fit your personality, your ambition level, and stir something inside that will inspire you to go out there and take charge of your life. Whether you want to make money, if you are unemployed or just plain tired of working for someone else, ideas are abundant.

Hopefully this list and these ideas will also get your own creative energy flowing and you may come up with brand-new ideas of your own. If you do, and you would like to share, I would love to hear from you.

Let's talk about the first batch of ideas:

Lawn care

Garage cleaning services

Cleaning windows

Pet sitting

Drivingly elderly

Buying and selling surplus stock from local businesses

Dog walker

Rent part of your lawn to gardeners

In-home care provider

Painting

Rubbish removal

Bargain hunting at tag sales

Participate in medical studies

Become a moving advertisement

Sell plasma, hair, and other ... things

We will go through each of these one at a time in more detail.

Lawn Care

If you have paid attention in the last 20 or 30 years, you'll have noticed a significant increase in the number of lawn care services that exist just about everywhere in this country.

Anywhere that people live and have their own lawns, more and more of them have less and less time to attend to it.

You would need a few things to get started, and you may already have everything you need.

Obviously, you would need a lawn mowing machine. This could be a push mower or riding tractor. Professional lawn services use walk behind mowers that allow them to save time and effort while taking care of lawns. However, you can get started by taking on a few small yards with a 19 or 21 inch push mower.

You would need a way to transport your mower to your client's home, but if you're going to start with a small 19 inch push mower, you can break that down to fit in the back of most trunks. You would also need a string trimmer. You can find a number of string trimmer's that are inexpensive at your local Home Depot or other lawn and garden supply shops.

If you want to do an exceptional job, make sure that you also pick up a leaf blower. This will allow you to blow off any grass that is thrown over sidewalks or driveways, making the presentation of the lawn, when you're done, exceptional. You can advertise by going door-to-door to your neighbors first or running an ad in your local paper.

Lawn care has become a very lucrative business that doesn't require a great deal of concentration. You do need to be safe and exercise common sense while working outdoors, but you would only be limited by your ambition and desire to take on a specific number of accounts. Just remember when pricing, you don't want to undervalue your effort or your work and you also do not want to overcharge because word will spread fast.

Determine how long it would take you to mow an average size lawn, how much you require to make per hour, and that should give you a rough estimate of how much to charge. You may also be able to speak with any number of lawn care professionals who don't operate within your area to inquire about what they charge for different sized lawns.

Garage Cleaning Services

If you have ever lived in a home with a garage, you know how quickly things can pile up in it. The garage is the one place for just about every piece of broken equipment, unfinished projects, and even outdoor equipment and furniture gets stored in here. Over the years, a garage can become so crowded with junk that the homeowner simply ignores it because they can't devote the time to go through everything.

These are wonderful opportunities that you can use to help make some extra money. You can agree, for a fair price, to go through and clean out garages. You would have to sit down and talk to the homeowner about what they might want to keep and what they are willing to let go of. They may agree to have you clean everything out, regardless of what it is. When this happens, you will often find a treasure trove of items that you could turn around and sell for either scrap or at a tag sale.

When you work as a garage cleaner, you have to make sure that you do the job as you specified it would be done and be completely honest about everything. If the homeowner agreed that you can take whatever you wanted from the garage, as long as it's clean when you're done, and you find a high priced tool, for example, the right thing to do is to let the homeowner know what you found and what you estimate its value to be. They may wish to keep it for themselves, and you may feel like you lost out on an opportunity, but you will be recognized for your honesty and that will spread from them to their friends and family members who then may want to hire you to do the same thing for them in their garage.

It can be incredibly difficult to figure out how much to charge for different garages. You cannot use a one price fits all approach. You would need to determine the level of work that would be required, how many hours you may need to devote to this particular project, and how many trips in your car or truck that you might have to take to the local town dump or scrap metal yard, and any fees that may be associated with it.

The best approach to agreeing on a price is to work out a system with the homeowner in which you work for a preset number of hours, and then have him or her inspect your progress where you can explain what you've done so far and what your total estimate will be. If the homeowner wishes to have you stop cleaning their garage, they would pay you for what you did and you would move on to the next project.

Most homeowners, when they see a section of garage that is spotless, will be inspired to have you continue your work as agreed to completion. You could potentially make anywhere between $100 and $200 a day operating your own garage cleaning service.

Cleaning Windows

One thing that people don't do well, or don't care to do, is clean windows. Homeowners often neglect their windows because they are often located in hard to reach areas from the outside. So they focus on cleaning their windows on the inside, but over time the dirt and residue builds on the outside of the glass and they lose the luster of the sparkling shine to their windows.

Businesses rarely have time to focus on their windows. They are too busy stocking shelves, serving customers, or tending to everyday tasks and don't consider windows to be a major concern. However, when customers see a business that has spotless windows, it gives the sense that this business cares.

When you set out to make money cleaning windows, you can target both businesses and residential customers alike. Let's say that you focus on homes to start. The average window will likely have two main panes of glass and one or two storm windows. To clean the inside as well the outside, you may need stepladders or full-sized ladders. That may require you to have a pickup truck or van on which to secure the ladders.

Set out one day to clean your own windows. Research the best way to clean windows and you will find that newspaper is much more effective than paper towels and a squeegee can cut your cleaning time by more than half. Practice on your own windows and time yourself. Time yourself from the moment you would've arrived at this house if it wasn't yours. Continue to do a few more windows, determining how long it takes to do each one, and you will have a gauge on how much you can make in an hour cleaning windows.

Some window cleaning services might charge five dollars per window or $10 per window, depending on how large the window is and how accessible it is. Window cleaning can be lucrative in much the same way that lawn care is because you would end up developing relationships with repeat customers. You may sell your services on a monthly basis to homeowners and a weekly or biweekly basis to business owners. Also, window cleaning services can be carried out throughout the year, regardless of the season.

Pet Sitting

If you love pets, you can start your own pet sitting business. There are numerous people who have to travel for business or personal reasons throughout the year, and they end up leaving their cats or dogs, their beloved pets, in kennels. This is something they would prefer not to do, but at the same time they might not have the opportunity to seek out professional pet sitters.

Using some elbow grease and clever marketing, you can make it known throughout your neighborhood that you have a professional pet sitting service. You will need to be presentable, professional, and be able to put your client at ease about leaving their pet in your care. You may not want or be able to have pets in your home, and if that's the case, you can provide your service to visit your client's home or even stay there with the pets.

As long as you remain professional and have exceptional references that can be verified, a person would be more comfortable having someone like you look after their pets in the comfort of their own home rather than dropping their beloved pets off at a kennel.

If your pet sitting service becomes quite popular, you may want to consider acquiring insurance for your new business. While you won't steal

from your clients because you are a professional,

there is always a possibility of damage occurring

to the property whether it is caused by you, the

pets you are looking after, or another reason.

You will be in their home so you will be liable

for any damage. So insurance is very important.

Driving the Elderly

There are numerous elderly individuals within

every community that have difficulty getting

around because they either cannot drive

themselves anymore or do not feel comfortable

with it. They may wait for the bus or rely on

local senior services to bring them to the mall or

to the supermarket, but they may want to go to other places including doctor visits, visiting friends, or going to stores that are not located in a mall or plaza.

You can offer your services to drive these elderly clients wherever they need to go throughout the day. You would want to base your rates on the amount of time that you will devote to picking them up, driving them wherever they want to go, waiting for them, and returning home, as well as the amount of gas that you use in the process.

The average reimbursement expense for employees when they drive company vehicles is

$.36 per mile. You can use an equivalent rate or something slightly lower. Taxicab companies today tend to charge not only for the mileage driven but also the time that they sit and wait. Those fees can add up in a hurry.

In order to charge the elderly for money, you are legally obligated to get a livery license from the DMV as well as insurance. Whether you do or not is up to you, and just like any business opportunity, you need to make decisions that protect yourself as well as provide you with the highest profit potential.

Buying and Selling Surplus Stock from Local Businesses

Many local businesses end up with more stock than they could sell, especially when new versions of what they're trying to sell are being released. Some of these businesses have arrangements with their suppliers to buy back their surplus stock, but for those businesses that don't have this arrangement, this can be a lucrative opportunity for you.

You can offer to buy back the surplus stock from these businesses at "cost" and then turn around and sell these items for a percentage profit through online auction sites, local ads in the paper, or even tag sales.

Some businesses would rather keep their surplus stock, assuming that they will eventually sell everything, but others would rather clear shelf space for new, more appealing items that their customers would be more likely to spend money on.

You can advertise your service in local publications that business leaders would read or simply go door-to-door to retail businesses explaining what you do and letting them know to contact you if they want to get rid of any of their surplus stock.

You would require a fair amount of startup capital because you would need to purchase the surplus stock items upfront and then make your money back when you turn around and sell them. If you do not have any capital to work with, you can put together a solid business proposal and present it to close friends and family members and asked them for any support they may be willing to give to get you started.

Rent Part of Your Lawn to Gardeners

One often overlooked money making opportunity for homeowners is to be able to rent part of your lawn out to local gardeners. Many people live in apartments or condominiums for a variety of reasons, yet they may miss being able to attend and grow their own garden because they do not have the space where they are.

If you have a large lawn, you can set up a number of different gardens for people in the neighborhood to come and tend to their own crops. This kind of business opportunity will provide you with a little extra cash, usually in the form of a monthly rent for the space, but you are not going to be able to retire on this kind of money.

Once you get a couple of people working gardens on your property, word will spread fast so you will need to set a limit on how much of

your lawn to devote to this business venture.

In-Home Care Provider

A word of caution if you want to become an in-

home care provider. Most states have strict

regulations regarding in-home care. However, if

you want to help people such as the elderly or

disabled live more independent lives, and won't

be required to attend to any medication needs or

any healthcare issues, then you can be an in-

home care provider.

You would essentially help take care of someone

who may have trouble taking care of themselves

in their home. This could involve cleaning

dishes, cooking for them, making sure that they can make it to the bathroom, helping them into bed, or even accompanying them on a walk.

If you are a people person, then this could be a great opportunity for you. Never mislead anybody into believing that you are a professional healthcare provider. Make sure that they know your services are only in the capacity as a companion and an assistant to their daily routines.

When you are an in-home care provider, the person that you are taking care of and helping out may bond with you. That may lead to a more personal connection, which could make it more difficult for you emotionally if you tend to care for the elderly and they pass away.

Dog Walker

In the beginning of this chapter, I mentioned dog walkers. While this service tends to be more popular in major metropolitan areas, even rural communities may require the services of a passionate and skilled dog walker.

If you have a love of dogs, are not intimidated by different kinds of breeds, and enjoy getting exercise, becoming a dog walker could be a great opportunity for you to make some extra money. Depending on where you live, this could be a full-time position or just part-time hours.

That doesn't mean that if you live in a rural area you wouldn't find enough work to keep you busy full-time, but it will be more challenging. The responsibilities for a dog walker are generally going to the owner's house and collecting dog, taking him or her for a walk, cleaning up after the dog, and getting it enough exercise to stay healthy.

Some people have dogs but are physically unable to take them for walks, while others may work far from home and it takes them away for 9, 10, or even more hours. For them, having somebody visit the home to take their beloved dog for a walk will be a great peace of mind.

Most dog walkers charge per dog per day.
Determining how much you should charge can
be done by calling professional dog walking
services in other major metropolitan areas.

Painting

Painters can make a tremendous amount of
money in a short amount of time. While the
process of painting is not a difficult one to learn
and master, you need to know the right kinds of
paint to use in different situations. You can learn
about this by picking up any number of short
books on the subject or searching the Internet
and watching videos from professional painters.

It is important to be able to work very neatly when you are a painter. Whether you are working in someone's home or business, you will be working around their personal possessions, as well as flooring such as carpeting or hardwood stained floors. The neater you work, the better your reputation will become.

In order to start as a painter, you will need some basic tools such as paintbrushes, drop cloths, rollers, and pans. Most professional painters use pickup trucks or vans so that they can keep all of the necessary tools on hand at all times. You will need to understand how to edge effectively, use painters tape, and make the paint on walls, ceilings, doors, frames, or anywhere else appear fluid and avoid stroke lines and patterns.

You may also need to have a stepladder or full-length extendable ladder on hand in case you have to reach challenging spots such as the upper walls of a stairwell. Competition for jobs as a painter will be tough, especially during tight economic times. Construction workers and contractors were the hardest hit during the Great Recession of 2008 through 2010. Many of these contractors had steady jobs but then turned to painting as a way to make some money in the interim.

Rubbish Remover

Lastly for this initial list of potential jobs that you can do is a rubbish remover. In a way this may seem similar to offering a garage cleaning service, but the major difference is that rubbish could be from any room, crawlspaces, basements, and even debris from the yard.

Most rubbish removers will have at least a pickup truck if not a larger vehicle with an open back dump body. You will not be able to effectively remove rubbish in the backseat of your Toyota.

The amount of money that you would charge for rubbish removal would depend on the type of rubbish that you are taking away, how much the local dump would charge for that service, and how important it is to your potential client to get rid of it. People tend to build piles of rubbish somewhere on the property so that they do not have to deal with it at the time. However, at some point they either realize that they can no longer avoid it or someone new has purchased the home and are working on cleaning it up.

There are quite a few rubbish removal companies throughout the country that make a decent amount of money providing this valuable service to homeowners.

Bargain Hunting at Tag Sales

If you have some extra money that you can use to invest, and you're not working or have a lot of extra time to spare, spend your weekends going around to tag and garage sales. During the week, estate sales can be great places to find bargains.

Go to these sales as early as possible and try to find some items that you believe would sell for far more than they are priced at the tag sale. Purchase these items and then go home and list them on Ebay, Craiglist, or another website where you can set a minimum price.

You will need to write a compelling description for each item, unless it essentially speaks for itself (such as a popular collector's item). Often, people hold tag sales to get rid of things they consider to be 'junk.' They might not know the true value of some of their items or are more concerned with getting rid of them than worrying about getting the most money for them.

Moving sales are also a great place to find amazing bargains. People who are moving tend to be more desperate to eliminate unnecessary and unwanted items from their possession. If they don't sell them, then they will have to pack and move them, or throw them away.

Always plan to haggle for items you find at these sales. You can also head back to them at the end of the day and make offers on whatever is left over. Make sure that you only pay a fraction of what you know you can get online. Then, after every sale you make, set aside a portion of the profits to go toward purchasing more items the following week.

Participate in Medical Studies

Becoming involved in medical studies can be a challenge, especially during tough economic times because there is generally a high level of interest. However, if you fit the requirements of a particular medical research study (ie., male, 25-45, active with no history of heart conditions), and you are selected, you can make a considerable amount of money with some of these studies.

Obviously you don't want to put your health at risk for any amount of money, and most of these research studies are controlled and completely safe. Some of them will offer a small amount of money for a short period of time while others can offer thousands of dollars to accepted participants but require you to remain committed to the study for several months.

Most of these studies are not advertised in traditional publications, so check with any universities, medical clinics, or other related venues within your area. For larger studies, make sure you'll be willing and able to commute to the facility for the duration of the study. If you drop out or miss an appointment, it could void the agreement and you may not receive any compensation as a result.

Become a Moving Advertisement

By simply placing an advertisement for a local business on your t-shirt, for example, you can make money. Go around town and solicit local business for some of their advertisement revenue. You will want to have a solid plan in place, showing them a few samples of well designed ads that highlight the benefits of visiting the business.

You'll need to invest in a few sample t-shirts and silk screening in the beginning of this endeavor (don't try and write the name of the business with a catchphrase in permanent marker). Be professional in your approach.

Let the business owner or manager know where you will wear this walking advertisement and for how long you will do it. Agree on a price that makes it worth your while to continue marketing for this business.

For example, you could develop a shirt for a local deli, advertising some of their most popular lunch specials, then walk along the block where people work between 11am and 1pm. This way, when people leave their office in search of food, they'll see your shirt and immediately think about heading to the deli you're advertising.

You can also wear this walking advertisement at the local mall. Why stop there? You could even solicit some mall stores to hire you and have you walk about the mall. This is especially helpful for small stores that are tucked out of the main thoroughfare of foot traffic.

With this money making idea, you can work just a few hours a day and make a fair amount of money.

Sell Plasma, Hair, and Other ... *Things*

Plasma, hair, and even other body fluids can be sold. Fertility clinics will purchase semen from healthy men and may also offer a considerable amount of money for harvest eggs from women. You can sell plasma (from your blood) every few weeks, though you're not going to make a great deal of money doing this. Still, every little bit helps.

If you have long hair and are looking for a change in style, consider selling your locks to a company that makes natural wigs. These natural wigs are often used for cancer patients and other individuals who have lost their hair due to medical conditions. You could perform a valuable service while making a few dollars on the side.

These are just a few of the many incredible ideas that exist that can provide you money when you're unemployed or offer you opportunities to become your own boss. Most of the opportunities listed here in this chapter are more of a physical type of work. In the next chapter, I am going to introduce opportunities that require more mental focus but can be done, primarily,

from the comfort of your home.

4 – More Ideas (for the Stay-at-Home Type)

I started with jobs that most people could begin

doing this very minute. Some of them require

equipment or startup capital, but they are easy

to learn and don't require a great deal of time to

become adept at them.

The following jobs in this chapter may require a

bit more of a learning curve. There are many

ways to improve one's understanding of the

different aspects that go into these types of jobs.

You can learn from online courses, video

tutorials, webinars, or even books published at

your local Barnes & Noble or other bookstores.

The more time you invest in learning about these different opportunities, the faster you will learn and be able to jump in and take advantage of them.

Some of these great opportunities are:

1. Affiliate marketing
2. Drop shipping products
3. Freelancing
4. Virtual admin assistant
5. Call center attendant
6. Writing e-books
7. Blogging for profit
8. Build websites to sell
9. Complete online surveys

So let's discuss these job opportunities now.

Affiliate Marketing

One of the most popular and lucrative opportunities that exist online is selling affiliate products. With this, you would sign up with a company that sells certain products and agree to market those products yourself. People would find your website or ads about those products and make purchases to the company, but you will be credited with the sale and earn a commission for that sale.

The fundamental key of affiliate marketing is that you need to make an investment of time and some money to build a presence online so that potential customers can find those products through your website or advertisements.

One of the major downfalls of affiliate marketing is that people do not understand that you are not going to make a great deal of money by marketing just one product. If you are interested in affiliate marketing, you should focus on a large number of products. However, you want to find a niche in which to operate. In other words, you don't want to try marketing an energy drink as well as denture adhesives. Instead, you want to focus on energy drinks and anything else that people who would drink these products would be interested in.

The more time that you spend working on getting attention for the products you are selling, the more products you are likely to sell. You can pick and choose which products that you would want to market, so you are not stuck by a company's decision about what to offer.

Avoid any affiliate products that require you to pay money upfront. Some companies do offer a package that provides you with a website, domain name, and a few other tools to get you started, but remember, trying to sell one product is not going to help you much in the long run. Try to focus on affiliate products that allow you to market other products alongside them. Also, do not attempt to go the Amazon route and carry everything under the sun. You will not be able to compete against the major retailers in the world so it's best to focus on a specific niche, preferably something you are passionate about.

Dropshipping Products

Thanks to dropshipping, you can establish your own retail company that sells an assortments of products, and you won't even need to keep any inventory on hand. With this type of endeavor, you would basically provide information about any products that you wish to offer your potential consumers and when they order a product, you collect the money and then forward their name and address to the dropshipping company and they send out the item(s).

You get to set the price for each item based on what the dropshipping company charges. After their cost and the shipping costs are deducted from the final sale price you've determined, that is what you make as a profit.

The best aspect about dropshipping is that you don't need any real startup capital, just some marketing savvy and the ability to connect with prospective customers. You can do this from your home computer any time you want. You can sell one or two items or hundreds, depending on your ambition and ability to maintain a website, post items on auction or classified ad sites, or develop a catalogue.

When it comes to dropshipping, how much you make is all up to you.

Freelancing

If you have a specific skill, such as writing, graphic design, or even programming, you can become a freelancer. Competition is fierce and it will require you to have a strong portfolio in order to make a significant amount of money. However, there are dozens of websites for freelancers that have clients who are willing to pay for their services. Here are a few them:

Odesk.com

Freelancer.com

Elance.com

Guru.com

When you freelance, there is no guarantee that you will get any jobs on a specific week. You may be awarded a dozen jobs one week and none the next. You need to be able to find the right balance to be able to support yourself and your family.

Modern freelancers not only compete with other providers from all over the world, but they also gain access to potential clients from all over the world. Clients could be individuals or major companies. You would need to know how much you are willing to charge for each service that you would provide, how much the industry standard is, and how much is reasonable based on your current portfolio of work.

If you do not have any kind of portfolio to show, then I suggest beginning by focusing on local businesses and offering your services either at an exceptionally low rate or pro bono just so that you can develop high-quality samples for your portfolio.

The more experience you have and the more samples of work that you've done, you will have a better opportunity of getting projects, and it will also allow you to charge a little bit more money when you could prove that your quality of work is better than average.

Virtual Admin Assistant

Virtual administrative assistants can offer small, independent businesses and contractors a valuable service. A virtual assistant is a person who could be living anywhere and still assist with many administrative tasks that a business has. Most likely you would need a fast Internet connection, a Skype account, and a computer with the ability to videoconference. Sometimes all you need is an email address.

Common tasks that are often involved in a virtual administrative assistant's job might be organizing schedules, answering phones, making phone calls, bookkeeping, and other general tasks and responsibilities that an in-house secretary would normally perform.

Virtual administrative assistants tend to work for businesses that are predominantly online oriented. Freelancers and independent contractors who deal with phone and email inquiries are the most common types of business owners who hire VAs.

The time requirements for VAs will vary, depending on the individual business needs.

Call Center Attendant

If you have ever called a company's customer service helpline, you have likely been connected to a call center attendant. While many of us have had the unpleasant experience of talking to someone who barely speaks our language, companies today are starting to turn to call center attendants that live within their country of operation (where their customers live and speak the language clearly).

To become a call center attendant, you would likely be hired by a firm that provides a service to major companies. You may have scripts and manuals for half a dozen or even more companies. A customer from any one of these companies would call the customer service hotline number and be patched through to your call center's firm. The number would be rerouted to your fault line based on availability and whether you are up next in the queue.

You would be able to determine the phone number being routed, what company the customer is trying to call, and you would need to answer the phone based on the script that company provides. The customer would ask questions or explain the issue on why they are calling and you would address their comments, concerns, or questions in the manner that you are trained with the scripts given.

Being a call center attendant can be a frustrating challenge, depending on the person you're talking to. You will most likely find part-time call center attendant opportunities to start, but may be able to increase your hours as you gain more experience.

Writing eBooks

E-books cost virtually nothing to publish today. However, you have to write the content that you want to sell. You can either write your e-books yourself or hire a ghostwriter to create them for you. The e-books should be on topics that you understand so that you can answer any questions that your potential readers may have.

E-books provide you with an opportunity of becoming an "authority" in your chosen field of expertise. They also provide you with an opportunity to make money. You can publish on a range of sites such as Amazon (for the Kindle), Barnes & Noble (for the Nook), and dozens of other sites. You will need to format your e-book differently for each platform, though most sites can now take MS Word documents (docx files) and convert them automatically into ePub, Kindle, Nook, and other formats.

You can charge almost anything you want for your e-books, but some sites have minimum limits for pricing and if you charge too much, you will struggle to make sales. One aspect of writing and selling e-books that too many authors neglect is marketing. Authors incorrectly assume that just because it's published, people will find it and buy it. With more than 250,000 new titles published in e-book format each year, getting noticed requires marketing.

You may write the best e-book in the world, but if people don't know about it, they can't buy it. Writing is only one aspect of selling e-books.

Blogging for Profit

Many businesses use blogging as a way to connect with their customers, provide valuable information, and become an authority on the products or services that they provide. Some of these businesses rely on professional bloggers to help them gain a wider audience and more customers.

If you enjoy writing, you can blog as well as video blog about topics that are important to you, of interest to your readers, and even those that cater to certain businesses. The more readers you get to your blog, the more power you end up having. When you have a lot of readers, companies will be willing to pay for your services and hire you to write blogs that would redirect your readers to their company websites.

The most important factor when it comes to blogging for profit is that if you are not passionate about writing, or if you are not very creative, you'll find it a very challenging prospect. Blogging for profit requires consistency and a devotion to your craft in the beginning, knowing that you will not make any real money when you first start out. Only when you have a loyal and consistent readership would you be able to make money through other businesses and even advertising on your blog.

Blogging today doesn't require any startup costs as you can obtain a free WordPress blog site or even a page on Blogger.com as well as many others. WordPress is fast becoming the universal choice for professional bloggers.

Build Websites to Sell

An often overlooked opportunity to make money is by building websites that you intend to sell. There are millions of websites and billions of webpages already in existence, but a vast majority of those websites do not attract attention and don't have visitors coming to the site.

If you have a passion for creating websites and driving traffic to those websites, you can begin building a wide variety of websites and marketing those websites to prospects. You may have information that you can use as your selling point, or products that you can sell through the website. The more visitors per month that you can acquire on each of these websites, the more valuable they become. When you have, for example, 10,000 visitors coming in every month, then other businesses and companies will likely have an interest in acquiring that website. After all, 10,000 visitors coming to the site is a significant number and hard to achieve.

Some entrepreneurs regularly build new websites with almost no start-up cost other than acquiring the domain address, and then learn how to become savvy marketers in order to drive traffic to their sites. They then turn around and sell these websites for a tidy profit and start the process all over.

Some people simply enjoy the process of creating websites and building them into popular forums. You can make a fair amount of money by selling successful websites.

Complete Online Surveys

Many large companies spend a great deal of money trying to determine what their potential customers will want. They go to great lengths to try and get people to fill out surveys, which is why they hire other companies to conduct them. These survey companies offer a couple of dollars and even more to people who are willing to fill out any number of surveys.

Filling them out can take time, be boring or confusing at times, but if you are willing to answer questions and give your opinion, then you can make some good money filling them out. The requirements for filling out surveys will often differ from one to the next, so you want to make sure you don't approach them the same or ignore the instructions. Many survey companies stipulate that they will not pay if you don't follow the instructions or complete the entire survey (every question).

You will likely be asked general rating questions (agree, somewhat agree, etc.) as well as open ended questions ('how do you feel about ...). Be sure to read each question carefully and give constructive opinions and feedback. The more surveys you complete, the more money you can make.

Conclusion

Being without a job can be a frustrating aspect of life. The longer you are without work, the more stress you will generally feel. Questions will begin to surface in your mind: How am I going to pay my bills? How can I support my family? Am I ever going to find work again?

The questions and the stress begin to mount and if you don't take charge, they can lead to depression, anxiety, and other emotional problems, not to mention driving you deeper into debt and causing you to lose what you worked so hard to attain.

However, even in the darkest moments of our lives, there is always light; sometimes you just need to know where to look in order to see it. Most of us tend to focus only on the types of jobs that we've had in the past when we're looking for work now. For example, if you've always been an administrative assistant, then those are the types of jobs that you look for in the help wanted section of the newspaper, right? Also, if you're been a middle manager for a while, then you're going to want to get a management job for your next employment opportunity.

And therein lies the main part of the problem; we spend so much time looking for the same type of jobs that we forget to think (or look) outside 'the box.' Yet as you can quickly and readily see from just a few of the ideas in this book, there are many, many ways to make money even when you're not working.

Break Out beyond Labels

Don't worry about what your college diploma (or lack of one) may say. Don't worry about the types of jobs that you've had in the past. Don't worry about how much money you made during your most recent employment. None of those aspects define who you are.

Do you think that a janitor who makes $40,000 a year is any less than a teacher making the same money? If so, you need to ask yourself why?

What difference does it make whether a person

cleans buildings for a living or teaches students?

Better yet, how would you rate a garbage man

making $25 an hour as opposed to someone who

hasn't worked in two years? Does it suddenly

matter what you do to make money?

Some of these opportunities aren't glamorous.

Some have the prospect of turning into careers.

And some are just temporary ways to make a

few extra bucks in the meantime. No matter

what you do to make money, it's still helping

you pay the bills. As long as it's legal, then what

difference does it make? Who's going to ridicule

you for that? If they do, that's their problem, not yours.

Now let's get moving and make some serious jobless cash!

Other Books Available By Author On Kindle, Audio and Paperback

The Killer Instinct: How To Master It and Achieve Anything That You Want

Winning Habits: Getting Rid of A Loser's Mentality

Conquering Your Fears

Passive Income: Stop Working Hard For Your Money And Let Your Money Work Hard For You

How To Create A Profitable Ezine From Scratch

The Secrets Of Making $10,000 on Ebay in 30 Days

The Complete Guide To Investing in Gold And Silver: Surviving The Great Economic Depression

How To Sell Any Product Online:"Secrets of The Killer Sales Letter"

How To Make A Fortune Using The Public Domain

Search Engine Domination: The Ultimate Secrets To Increasing Your Website's Visibility And Making A Ton Of Cash

Creative Real Estate Investing Strategies And Tips

How to Make Money Online:"The Savvy Entrepreneur's Guide To Financial Freedom"

How to Overcome Your Self-Limiting Beliefs & Achieve Anything You Want

The Secrets of Finding The Perfect Ghostwriter For Your Book

The Creative Real Estate Marketing Equation: Motivated Sellers + Motivated Buyers = $

How To Start An Online Business With Less Than $200

How To Market Your Business Online and Offline

Money Blueprint: The Secrets To Creating Instant Wealth

Affiliate Cash: How To Make Money As An Affiliate Marketer

How To Promote Market And Sell Your Kindle Book

AudioBook Profits: How To Make Money by Turning Your Kindle, Paperback and Hardcover Book into Audio.

The Fine Art of Writing The Next Best Seller on Kindle

Fast Cash: 9 Amazing Ways To Make Money Without Having To Work At A Job

Money Magnet: How to use the Laws of the Universe to Attract Money into Your Life

Hypnotic Influence: How To Create A Cult Like Following For Anything That You Do

The Art of Manipulation: How to Get Anybody to Do What You Want